Y0-EGD-672

SEA SNAKES

SEA MONSTERS

HOMER SEWARD

The Rourke Press, Inc.
Vero Beach, Florida 32964

PHOTO CREDITS
All photos © Marty Snyderman; except © Lynn M. Stone: pages 18, 19

EDITORIAL SERVICES:
Penworthy Learning Systems

Library of Congress Cataloging-in-Publication Data

Seward, Homer. 1942-
    Sea snakes / by Homer Seward.
        p. cm. — (Sea monsters)
    Includes index
    Summary: Describes different kinds of snakes that live in the sea, discussing their physical characteristics, venom, habitats, habits, and relationships with people.
    ISBN 1-57103-240-1
    1. Sea snakes—Juvenile literature [1. Sea snakes. 2. Snakes.] I. Title. II. Series: Seward, Homer, 1942-   Sea monsters.
QL666.0645S48 1998
597.96'177—dc21   98–20296
                                                                          CIP
                                                                          AC

Printed in the USA

TABLE OF CONTENTS

SEA SNAKES

Not all snakes live on land or in swamps and rivers. Highly poisonous sea snakes, big and small, live in and near some of the world's warm seas.

Don't worry, you won't find them in the warm waters of the coastal United States.

Many sea snakes spend part of their lives on land. A second group of sea snakes, however, are truly **marine** (muh REEN) snakes. They never leave the ocean.

A turtlehead sea snake slips through the warm blue sea.

SEA SNAKES AS SEA MONSTERS

Real sea monsters don't exist, of course; but any sea animal that's scary or dangerous can be called a sea monster.

An olive sea snake glides along the sea bottom as it hunts for fish.

They're not monsters, but sea snakes pack a deadly bite.

Sea snakes can be scary because they are very dangerous. They make **venom** (VEN um), or poison, that is extremely powerful. Their venom can easily kill their **prey** (PRAY), the creatures that sea snakes eat.

Sea snake venom can also kill people. But, sea snakes and people rarely come in contact.

WHAT SEA SNAKES LOOK LIKE

The most **aquatic** (uh KWAT ik), or water-loving, sea snakes have flat tails for swimming power. All sea snakes have small eyes and nostrils they can close to keep water out.

Sea snakes come in many colors—plain, spotted, and banded.

Some sea snakes have smooth skin. Others have rough or spiny skin.

Most sea snakes are two and a half feet (nearly one meter) to six feet (two meters) long. The largest is Stokes's sea snake. It is six feet (two meters) long and 10 inches (25 centimeters) around.

This banded sea snake will leave the sea and spend part of its time on shore.

WHERE SEA SNAKES LIVE

The greatest number of sea snakes live in the warm ocean waters of Australia and southern Asia. The yellow-bellied sea snake travels from South America to South Africa!

Five kinds of sea snakes spend part of their lives on land and part at sea. Two **species** (SPEE sheez), or kinds, live in Asian lakes. Long ago, those lakes had outlets to the sea, and the sea snakes swam in from the ocean.

Many sea snakes like shallow water, but others can be found hunting in water over 150 feet (46 meters) deep.

A sea snake swims over a colorful reef in the Indian Ocean.

HABITS OF SEA SNAKES

The water-loving group of sea snakes spend their entire lives at sea. They are helpless on land.

These sea snakes bear their babies alive in the sea. The babies of other sea snakes are hatched from eggs laid on shore.

A golden sea snake snacks on a fish it caught on an Australian reef. The biggest snakes of this species reach six feet (two meters) in length.

Like snakes on land, sea snakes outgrow old skins and shed them in the sea.

Most sea snakes feed on fish. Some species hunt eels, which they pull from eel holes in the sea floor. Two types of sea snakes live almost completely on fish eggs.

SEA SNAKE VENOM

Some sea snakes have venom that is many times more deadly than a cobra's.

Many sea snakes use venom only to protect themselves from attack. The sea snakes that eat fish eggs use venom only in **self-defense** (SELF duh FENTS). They certainly don't have to kill fish eggs!

Many species also use venom to kill their prey, rather than for defense.

Sea snakes have small, round heads, unlike the broad, triangle-shaped heads of rattlesnakes and cottonmouths.

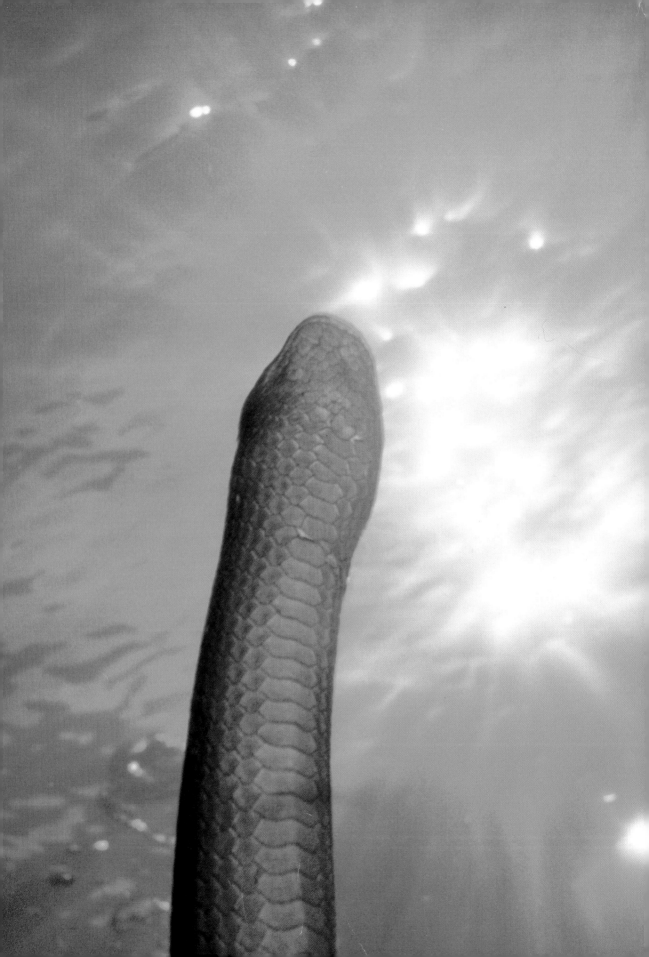

KINDS OF SEA SNAKES

Scientists know 53 species of sea snakes. Five are partly aquatic. The remaining 48 species are aquatic.

The partly aquatic species often spend time on land near the sea. They hide in caves or in cracks between rocks. These species, like the yellow-lipped sea snake, visit the water only to hunt.

One of the oddest sea snakes is the yellow-bellied. This snake's long journeys are remarkable. The snake doesn't swim so much as it floats. The yellow-bellied sea snake lets the current of the ocean move it along.

The olive sea snake is one of more than 50 species of snakes, most of which live in the tropical seas of Australia and Southern Asia.

THE SEA SNAKE'S COUSINS

Snakes, along with turtles, lizards, alligators, crocodiles, and tuataras (too uh TAHR uhs) are reptiles. Sea snakes are among the few reptiles that live in salt water.

The American coral snake shares the small, round head and deadly venom of its sea snake cousins.

The king cobra is a cousin of the sea snake, but sea snake venom is, ounce for ounce, more deadly than the cobra's.

The sea snake's closest cousins are some of the other venomous snakes, including cobras and mambas. The coral snake is the sea snake's closest relative in North America.

Sea snakes and their deadly cousins bite and chew to poison prey. Several other venomous snakes, such as rattlers, stab with their teeth.

SEA SNAKES AND PEOPLE

Sea snakes sometimes cause human death. Usually, a sea snake bites only when it has been frightened.

Most human deaths seem to be caused by the blue-ringed sea snake of the Phillipine Islands, Persian Gulf, and Japan.

Local people capture banded sea snakes on shore. They use the snakes for food and for their skins. In some parts of Asia, sea snake meat is a special treat.

A diver watches closely as a sea snake swims near.

GLOSSARY

aquatic (uh KWAT ik) — of the water; living on or in the water

marine (muh REEN) — of or relating to the ocean

prey (PRAY) — an animal that is hunted by another animal for food

self-defense (SELF duh FENTS) — that which an animal does to protect itself from harm

species (SPEE sheez) — within a group of closely related animals, one certain kind, such as a *yellow-lipped* sea snake

venom (VEN um) — a poison produced by certain animals, including the sea snake

Banded sea snake swims over a colorful Indian Ocean reef.

INDEX

FURTHER READING

Find out more about sea snakes with these helpful books:
Collard, Sneed B. *Sea Snakes.* St. Martins, 1993.
McCarthy. *Reptile.* Knopf, 1991.